Why Mockingbird Sings Many Songs

A Folktale From the Navajo

One day Mockingbird flew about the desert. He was in the land of the Navajo people. He was the only bird with gray feathers.

Mockingbird said, "The other birds have bright feathers. Their feathers are as bright as the sunrise. My coat is dull. It's as dull as the shadows at night. No one will see me. No one will think I am beautiful."

3

Wind Spirit heard
Mockingbird. He whispered,
"I can't change your gray coat.
But I will give you a string of
feather beads. You can wear it
around your neck."

Mockingbird listened. He
looked around for Wind Spirit.
He saw nothing. Spirits can't
be seen.

"Each bead has a different
song," said Wind Spirit. "You
may wish to share the beads.
There are enough for most of
the other birds."

Wind Spirit left with a great
WHOOSH! Mockingbird had a
wonderful necklace around his
throat.

Mockingbird picked a feather bead. He opened it. A song came to him. Mockingbird began to sing. It was lovely. The other birds gathered around.

"Teach us that song, Mockingbird!" they cried.

Mockingbird was happy with his new gift. He wished to share it.

"I have many songs on my feather necklace. I can never sing all of them," he said.

He began to give away feathers to the other birds. He gave away feather after feather after feather.

Poor Mockingbird got carried away! Before he knew it, he had given all the feathers away. One by one, the birds flew off. Each sang a different song. Each song was beautiful.

"Oh, no!" cried Mockingbird. "I have no song left to call my own."

He sat on a branch. He was silent. He listened to the songs of the other birds.

Wren saw that Mockingbird was not singing.

"Sing, Mockingbird!" he said. "Be happy with us."

"I can't sing," Mockingbird said sadly. "I gave all my songs away. Now I can only sit and listen."

Wren flew away. He told the other birds about Mockingbird. One by one, they grew silent.

Whippoorwill said to Mockingbird, "Take back your song feathers. It's not fair. We should not have all your feathers. Wind Spirit gave them to you."

"No," said Mockingbird. "You all sound beautiful. I could never take away your songs. Give me a tiny bit from each feather bead. Maybe I will be able to sing a little of each song."

That is just what the birds did. And that is why the Navajos call Mockingbird *Zah-ha-lunnie*. His name means "bird of many voices."

　　To this day, Mockingbird can't sing a song of his own. He sings a part of every other bird's song. Mockingbird can sing the most songs of all because he was kind to the other birds.